LET'S LEARN ADVERBS!

QUICKLY!

BY KATE MIKOLEY

Gareth Stevens
PUBLISHING

Please visit our website, www.garethstevens.com. For a free color catalog of all our high-quality books, call toll free 1-800-542-2595 or fax 1-877-542-2596.

Cataloging-in-Publication Data

Names: Mikoley, Kate.
Title: Let's learn adverbs! / Kate Mikoley.
Description: New York : Gareth Stevens Publishing, 2019. | Series: Wonderful world of words | Includes glossary and index.
Identifiers: LCCN ISBN 9781538218853 (pbk.) | ISBN 9781538218839 (library bound) | ISBN 9781538218860 (6 pack)
Subjects: LCSH: English language–Adverb–Juvenile literature.
Classification: LCC PE1325.M57 2019 | DDC 428.2'4–dc23

Published in 2019 by
Gareth Stevens Publishing
111 East 14th Street, Suite 349
New York, NY 10003

Copyright © 2019 Gareth Stevens Publishing

Designer: Katelyn E. Reynolds
Editor: Emily Mahoney

Photo credits: Cover, p. 1 TinnaPong/Shutterstock.com; p. 5 Karl Weatherly/Taxi/Getty Images; p. 7 Littlekidmoment/Shutterstock.com; p. 9 Kristina Zhuravleva/Shutterstock.com; p. 11 Soloviova Liudmyla/Shutterstock.com; p. 13 Vitpho/Shutterstock.com; p. 15 JARRUVAT HOMTHONG/Shutterstock.com; p. 17 spass/Shutterstock.com; p. 19 2xSamara.com/Shutterstock.com; p. 21 Rawpixel.com/Shutterstock.com.

Printed in the United States of America

CPSIA compliance information: Batch #CS18GS: For further information contact Gareth Stevens, New York, New York at 1-800-542-2595.

CONTENTS

Boldface words appear in the glossary.

What Are Adverbs?

Adverbs are words that **describe** other words, such as verbs. Verbs are action words, like *run* and *jump*. Adverbs tell us more about these kinds of words. Are you ready to learn all about adverbs? Check your answers on page 22.

Answering Questions

How? When? Where? Adverbs can answer questions like these! Look at the sentence below:

The family walks quickly.

Here, "quickly" is an adverb that tells us how the family does something. What verb does this adverb describe?

Adverbs can also tell us when something happened. They give more **information** on timing. Look at the following sentence:

It rained yesterday.

In this case, "rained" is the verb. What is the adverb that tells us when it rained?

9

Adverbs help us find out where something happened, too. *Here*, *there*, and *everywhere* are all words that can be used as adverbs. They help us figure out **location**. What is the adverb in the sentence below?

My dad drove us there.

Descriptive Words

Adverbs can also describe other adverbs or adjectives. Adjectives are words that describe nouns or **pronouns**. In the sentence below, "truck" is a noun. "Red" is an adjective that describes the truck. What is the adverb in this sentence?

Look at the bright red truck.

Super Suffix

Many adverbs end with the **suffix** "-ly." These two letters can turn an adjective into an adverb! For example, *slow*, *quiet*, and *happy* are often used as adjectives. However, *slowly*, *quietly*, and *happily* are adverbs. The adverb "slowly" describes how the snail is moving.

Adverb or Adjective?

Some words can be adverbs and adjectives. Look at the following sentence: **That was a hard test.** Here, "hard" is an adjective that describes the test. Now look at this sentence: **I worked hard on the test.** Here, "hard" is an adverb that describes how you worked.

17

Giving Meaning

Adverbs can change what a sentence means. The only difference in the sentences below is the adverb, but the meanings are very different. Which sentence describes the picture on the next page?

1. Jake angrily kicked the ball.

2. Jake joyfully kicked the ball.

Find Your Adverb

Can you think of more adverbs? You already use some every day without thinking twice. The next time you're doing something, think about how, where, or when you're doing it. That will help you find an adverb to describe it!

CHEERFULLY

21

GLOSSARY

describe: to say what something is like

information: facts about something

location: a place

pronoun: a word (such as I, you, he, she, it, they, or we) used in place of a noun

suffix: a letter or a group of letters added to the end of a word that changes the meaning of the word

ANSWER KEY

p. 6: walks

p. 8: yesterday

p. 10: there

p. 12: bright

p. 18: 2

FOR MORE INFORMATION

BOOKS

Ganeri, Anita. *Describing Words: Adjectives, Adverbs, and Prepositions.* Chicago, IL: Heinemann Library, 2012.

Loewen, Nancy. *The Big Problem (and the Squirrel Who Eventually Solved It): Understanding Adjectives and Adverbs.* North Mankato, MN: Picture Window Books, 2016.

Murray, Kara. *Adjectives and Adverbs.* New York, NY: PowerKids Press, 2014.

WEBSITES

The Adverb
www.chompchomp.com/terms/adverb.htm
Use this site to learn more about these awesome words.

What Are Adverbs?
www.grammar-monster.com/lessons/adverbs.htm
Find out more about adverbs here.

INDEX

Public Library
DeKalb, Illinois
RULES

1. Books may be retained for two weeks and may be renewed once for the same period unless otherwise indicated.
2. A fine is charged for each day that library material is overdue.